Sorrow and Preaching at Funerals

C000254125

Nick Watson

Rector of Breadsall
Derby Diocesan Warden of Readers

GROVE BOOKS LIMITED
RIDLEY HALL RD CAMBRIDGE CB3 9HU

Contents

The Cover Illustration is by Peter Ashton

First Impression June 2001
ISSN 0144-171X
ISBN 1 85174 467 3

1
Introduction[1]

The opening words of Ian Bunting's earlier Grove book on this subject are as true as they were in 1978. Only the appropriateness of the language has changed, with changes in ministry and English usage.

> No occasion offers a greater challenge to the sensitive pastoral preacher than the funeral service. Whether he knows the family of the deceased or not, he cannot hope to fathom the deep personal feelings with which they come to church. He is moreover president at a service which confronts him with questions about his own calling. Is he there as a folk priest to help the bereaved through this ancient rite of passage, or is he an apostle with good news to bring of God's eternal purpose for men and women? Most ministers will see themselves as both. They proclaim the hope of resurrection in Christ but they cannot do it in total disregard for the context in which they speak.[2]

Working with Readers in the Diocese of Derby, I have found again and again that, asked 'what are the most satisfying areas of your ministry?' those who minister in bereavement care and presiding at funerals will place this area of work close to the top of their lists. There may be many reasons for this. One, I am sure, is that when Christian ministers help people through the process of bereavement and funeral, we are meeting a need of which the bereaved are acutely aware. In contrast, in much of the rest of our work, we are often trying to meet a need to know God which others do not recognize that they have.

Having said that, while this area of ministry may be satisfying, it is far from easy, and finding 'the right words' for the sermon can seem impossible. This booklet is written in the hope of offering some ideas to help our reflection on what we are doing in preaching at a funeral, and how we might go about that task.

---

1 I encountered one difficulty early in the writing of this booklet. What terms should we use? Of the one who has died, 'deceased' and 'departed' both have considerable history, but both carry considerable weight and presuppose some theology—what, after all, has indeed ceased? And is the one who has died to be categorized solely by reference to his or her absence from the current experience of those still living? For that matter, how do we refer to those who attend the funeral? In one sense, they are (usually) properly referred to as *mourners*, but their position, certainly their identity, is far wider. They are also *congregation*, *bereaved*, and many more titles, both as a body and as individuals.
  I mention this difficulty not only to explain any following variation in terminology, but also for a more profound reason which is worth our examining at the outset. You may wish to ask yourself what terms *you* would naturally use of the different participants in the funeral, and to watch your use of those terms in practice; at times one may be appropriate, at times another.
2 *Preaching at Funerals*, Ian Bunting (Grove Ministry and Worship booklet W 62) p 3.

2

A Brief Look at the Service

Part of the stimulus to the writing of a new Grove booklet on preaching at funerals is the authorization for the Church of England of the *Common Worship* (CW) range of resources for funeral ministry. Some of what follows will be applicable to funeral ministry in general, but some comments will relate more specifically to preaching in the context of this liturgy.

Having said that, for a general treatment of the CW funeral service and resources, and of the wider CW project, you need to look elsewhere.[3] Here we are concerned with the way in which the liturgical setting might influence our preaching.

One characteristic which does affect us is the growing recognition that, as death and bereavement are processes which vary from one instance to another, so must be the church's ministry, in its liturgical aspect as much as in its pastoral. A quick page-count shows something of the development. The *Book of Common Prayer* (BCP) provided a single service (10 pages in my edition) for *The burial of the dead*. The *Alternative Service Book* (ASB) provided a total of 57 pages of resources for this ministry. These included readings for the time of death and distinct forms of prayer for the funeral of a child, for prayers after neonatal death, for the interment of ashes and for use before a funeral. CW provides 188 pages, covering the process from 'Ministry at the time of death' to 'Memorial Service: A Sample Service,' with a good range of prayers, readings and canticles to suit most situations. To make the best pastoral use of these resources and of our preaching, we will need to look later at how the two can be brought together, so that what is preached and what is prayed work together.

Another change which affects us is that in the way in which the funeral service is intended to fit into and move along the process of coming to terms with bereavement. The BCP emphasizes our universal mortality, and into that mortality proclaims the hope of resurrection. There is then no prayer to commend the departed to God, only the committal of the body and prayers for the coming of God's kingdom. The ASB countered this with an emphasis, from the opening prayer onwards, on the confidence of the Christian hope. The principal acknowledgement of the pain of the bereaved (in the liturgical text) is in the optional prayers. CW takes a different approach, expressing within the liturgy a degree of movement. This is demonstrated by a comparison of the opening prayers of the two modern rites.[4]

---

3   See the 'Further Reading' section at the end of this booklet.
4   BCP has no opening prayer.

Alternative Service Book

> Heavenly Father,
> in your Son Jesus Christ
> you have given us a true faith and a sure hope.
> Strengthen this faith and hope in us all our days,
> that we may live as those who believe in
> the communion of saints,
> the forgiveness of sins,
> and the resurrection to eternal life;
> through your Son Jesus Christ our Lord.
> Amen.

Common Worship

> God of all consolation,
> your Son Jesus Christ was moved to tears
> at the grave of Lazarus his friend.
> Look with compassion on your children in their loss;
> give to troubled hearts the light of hope,
> and strengthen in us the gift of faith,
> in Jesus Christ our Lord.
> Amen.

CW retains the ASB's confident and corporate prayer, but places it at the end of the service. It begins with the recognition before God of a shared grief, and draws Jesus' own experience into the sharing of that loss. This marks an important characteristic of the new liturgy, which significantly affects the place of the sermon. The CW service begins in present experience and present reality—the immediate awareness of the life that has come to an end, and of the shared pain of the mourners. The readings and sermon provide a 'hinge' around which the focus of the service turns, from mourning to hope. If the service is to 'flow' and help the process of grief, the sermon must do its job here. It is in this context that we must think and plan.

3

Principles

Our preaching in any context has to be shaped by our understanding of what we are doing, and preaching at a funeral is, if anything, a case for more reflection rather than less. So first, what is the purpose of the funeral service? That, after all, is the setting in which we are preaching, and knowing what we are trying to do is the best first step to doing it well.

We need to distinguish the aims of the funeral in two directions. First, there are those aspects of the service which are about the transition of an individual from life to death. Then there are the needs of the living, particularly those closest to the dead person, and the congregation.

Towards the Departed

At the most basic, functional level, the funeral service is about the properly reverent disposal of the body of a dead human being. It may seem that this is an obvious statement, but there is much about modern funeral practice which seems to be an attempt to conceal this brute fact, with its acknowledgement of the reality of death. It is not only the association with tradition which means that this element is expressed most eloquently at a service of burial in the churchyard. The undeniable physicality of the lowering of the coffin into the earth, as the minister speaks the sonorous 'earth to earth, ashes to ashes, dust to dust'[5] has a powerful impact in a way that the closing of a curtain in the crematorium chapel does not. But what does this have to do with preaching? Principally that, at most funerals, the sermon is preached in the presence of the body of the deceased. This requires some acknowledgement, and also affects the delivery of the sermon—to which we shall return.

Another aspect of the funeral, not explicit in BCP but plain in more recent liturgies, is that of the commendation of the person who has died to the care of God. There is room for considerable debate over the nature of this commendation, perhaps reflected in the range of optional commendation prayers provided! Most Christians would affirm that the person whose funeral we observe has already faced judgment in so far as he or she will do so before the end of time. If this be the case, then it might seem that our prayer for him or her is redundant by the time of the funeral (CW also provides prayers of commendation for use at the time of death, which are provided for a very different situation and take a different form).[6] At the very least, a prayer of

---

5   These words were made optional in ASB, but are required in CW. The latter also provides a variety of forms of words, reflecting the growing variety of funeral practice and the popularity of cremation followed by the interment of ashes.
6   *Pastoral Services*, pp 375–377, contrasting with those at the time of the funeral on pp 267 and 373–375.

commendation answers the human need of the mourners to let go emotionally of one who has died, releasing that one into the care of God. What must be made clear in discussion and planning of the funeral service is that this prayer is one which acknowledges a present (or at least implied) reality, rather than one which will achieve for the dead a state of rest or bliss otherwise unattained.

Towards the Bereaved

The second focus of the service is on the bereaved. Here there is a need to find the right balance between pastoral care and evangelism. This is not to imply that the two are in any way opposed, but they may well cause different emphases. On the pastoral side, a human need is fulfilled as we are enabled to say a last farewell to the person who has died. For those whose beliefs are shaped by Christianity, the message of the conquest of death can also bring comfort and hope. Mourners, whatever their degree of belief, can also find valuable support not only in the explicitly Christian content of the funeral liturgy, but also in the presence of friends and family.

On the side of evangelism, there is the ever-present duty of the Christian minister to make the good news of God's love known, in a way which is appropriate both to the situation and to the truth of the gospel. This requires finding the right way in which sensitively to introduce the concept of merciful judgment, as well as the overriding sense of forgiveness and hope.

The ministry which we exercise towards the bereaved in the funeral service includes, of course, the effect of that which we are seen to be exercising together towards the departed. The sense that we are accompanying the deceased on this last earthly stage of their journey is a powerful one, and may in itself be of considerable effect, if the service is structured so as to involve the mourners rather than to leave them as passive spectators.

4

The Christian Hope

Here we need to be careful. The ideas which many people assume to be 'Christian' around this area can be distorted and potentially harmful. The balance of pastoral sensitivity and faithfulness to what we believe can be very difficult to find and maintain when we are dealing with people in mourning, people at their most vulnerable. Clearly, the sermon at a funeral will not, and should not try to, answer all possible misconceptions, particularly those on which the family currently depend to keep going. But through pastoral care, the planning of the whole service and the sermon in particular, it is important not to encourage any mistaken ideas on 'the afterlife.' I have come across two main kinds of 'partially correct' ideas here. Some fall into the category of 'compulsory heaven for all,' and others rely on a hope of survival, rather than on one of resurrection. Each has its typical signs which arise during discussion of the deceased and the funeral service.

Heaven for Everyone!

A phrase which I have come to dread when visiting before funerals is 'Well, Vicar, he wasn't a religious man but...' usually followed by a few virtues attributed to the deceased. I have yet to meet anyone in these circumstances who believes in heaven yet seems to have considered the possibility that the one they mourn may not be there. Put like this, it seems a very bald statement. Clearly those who mourn faithful Christians have no reason to doubt this. The majority, though, simply have no idea that God's judgment is a reality, and that it is only through Jesus that we can hope with confidence for heaven.

This clearly requires the utmost sensitivity and work outside the funeral. In liturgy there has been a long tradition of the 'charitable assumption' that our words are personally valid. In referring to the deceased we speak and pray assuming faith, just as in baptism we assume that godparents making baptismal promises understand and affirm what they say, or at Communion we assume that those who confess their sins and receive absolution truly repent and desire God's forgiveness. In preaching, it will seldom be appropriate to challenge this assumption, but we must surely ensure that our words do not confirm it where it is clearly unwarranted. It may sometimes be possible and appropriate to speak in general terms of the Christian hope, without specifically referring to the presumed state of the deceased. This may preserve our own honesty, but we need to be cautious. On the one hand we risk seeming impersonal if this caution is not balanced by clear reference to the deceased elsewhere. On the other hand, we need to remember that the text of a funeral sermon is not going to receive a dispassionate analysis. What is heard may not be exactly what is said, and mourners may well read into our words

8

a personal assurance which we do not intend to be there.

There is clearly no one right answer—we are dealing with the delicate balance of pastoral sensitivity and integrity, and each of us must find the point of balance at which we are comfortable—or, perhaps, at which we are least uncomfortable!

Death is Nothing at All...

A second area of concern is characterized by the non-biblical reading I have found to be most frequently requested at funerals, of faithful Christians and of those 'on the fringe.' It is the famous piece by Henry Scott Holland.

> Death is nothing at all. I have only slipped away into the next room.
> I am I, and you are you: whatever we were to each other, that we are still.
> Call me by my old familiar name, speak to me in the easy way which you always used.
> Put no difference into your tone: wear no forced air of solemnity or sorrow.
> Laugh as we always laughed at the little jokes we enjoyed together.
> Play, smile, think of me, pray for me.
> Let my name be ever the household word that it always was.
> Let it be spoken without effort, without the ghost of a shadow on it.
> Life means all that it ever meant.
> It is the same that it ever was: there is absolutely unbroken continuity.
> What is this death but a gateway?
> I am but waiting for you, for an interval, somewhere very near just around the corner.
> All is well.[7]

These words, from a sermon on 1 John 2.2–3, were published in 1919, shortly after Scott Holland's death. The First World War had called into question many of the received ideas about the proper 'British' reaction to death. The sheer scale and pointlessness of the carnage had led to a rise in the practice of praying for the dead, and traditional beliefs about the place of death in the natural order of life had been shattered, along with liberal ideas of a gradual human progress towards perfection.

Doubtless Scott Holland's words brought comfort to some when they were preached, and to many when they were published. They still do bring comfort to many thousands year after year. But I would contend that their comfort is not one based upon authentic Christian hope. Rather it is based upon a minimizing of the impact of death. To say that 'death is nothing at all' is to play down the impact of bereavement, let alone the impact (still beyond our experience) of death itself. To those with a strong, if unclear, belief in the afterlife, these words may be of encouragement. Indeed they resonate with some

7 An extract from 'The King of Terrors,' a sermon on 1 John 3.2, 3. See *Facts of the Faith*—a collection of previously unpublished sermons by Henry Scott Holland edited by Christopher Cheshire (Longmans, 1919) p 126. A fuller extract can be found at http://www.grazweb.cwc.net/grazweb/holland/hsh-index.html

'New Age' ideas about the survival of the spirit. But they still clash with the experience of most who have lost family and friends. Indeed, I have found several times that the underlying belief, that death is of little significance, is one which many Christian people feel that they *ought* to share. It is as if people feel that genuine faith knows that death has been conquered, and so they ought not to grieve, knowing that they will be reunited with the one they have loved in this life. I have then seen the failure to approach bereavement with such equanimity become a source of felt guilt.

This attitude is, though, far from that of Jesus himself. I believe that one of the most telling passages in the gospels concerning death is that which tells of the raising of Lazarus, (John 11.1–44). Strangely, Jesus on hearing of Lazarus' illness waits until his friend has died before going to his aid. But then he stands at the tomb and weeps. Why, when surely he knew that he would shortly call Lazarus out of the tomb to life? The fact that he had deliberately waited for Lazarus' death argues against any suggestion that his action was a spontaneous response to his grief at the loss of a friend. If this was in Jesus' plan, why the sorrow? Would it not have been better to give the disciples an object lesson in the irrelevance of death by assuring them that all is well, and then calling forth Lazarus? Jesus' public grieving speaks of the reality of the pain of death, even to those who have full assurance of the conquest of death. Jesus, after all, knew exactly what was about to happen. Yet still he wept.

Death in the biblical revelation is an enemy, and among the greatest enemies, of human life. Death enters the story early, at the Fall. Paul assures us that of all the foes to be put under the feet of the victorious Christ, death is 'the last enemy to be destroyed.' This is *not* 'nothing at all.' However much comfort may be brought by Scott Holland's words, they do not have sufficient contact with the reality of human experience or with the reality of the biblical witness to be a secure basis for life in the face of death. For this reason I am always reluctant to use them at a funeral unless I have been able to explore their meaning with the mourners beforehand. I would also counsel care that whatever we say in preaching, and whatever we do liturgically at a funeral, does not reinforce our society's preference for the minimizing of the pain of death and bereavement. Too much of our language aids the effort to avoid acknowledging the impact of death. 'Passed on,' 'fallen asleep,' 'departed' are all easier to face than 'dead.' Indeed it has been commented that the set text of the funeral service in CW does not actually say explicitly that the person at the heart of the process is dead. A member of the liturgical commission in conversation said that they had rather assumed this was a shared understanding. On one level it is undoubtedly so, but on another level the reality of death may be denied. It is best to be clear about what the 'shared understanding' is at a funeral, lest we collude with a cosmetic support for the bereaved which actually gives them no solid ground on which to reconstruct life in the absence of the one who has died.

The popularity of Scott Holland's words, and the beliefs which underlie them, reflect a widespread understanding that the Christian hope is one of the survival of death. In its more developed form, this is the belief in an intrinsically immortal soul, which is the essential reality of the human person and which is housed for the duration of this life in a physical body. This view might be supported by reference to the language of 'putting aside the tent of the body' in 2 Peter 1.13–14. However, such a body-soul dualism seems to go against the main tenor of the biblical writing. If anything, it derives its character from Neo-Platonic ideas of the spiritual ideal in contrast to the physical and corrupting reality. The biblical hope which develops throughout the Testaments is not one of survival, but of resurrection. Eternal life is not an intrinsic property of our ethereal soul. It is the gift of God through Jesus Christ.

Resurrection—the Biblical Hope

This resurrection hope developed only gradually throughout the biblical period. The main texts in the OT fall into two categories.

1. An individual assurance of standing before God after death (Job 14.12–15; 19.25–27; Psalm 16.9–11; 49.15; implicit in Hosea 13.14).
2. An eschatological hope of the defeat of death and a general resurrection to judgment and then everlasting life or eternal shame (Isaiah 25.8; 26.19; Daniel 12.2, 3, 13).

A reading of these texts does not suggest an ethereal survival, but a fleshly resurrection—perhaps most clearly in Job 19.25–27. Further, this is always seen as a direct act of God, not as a natural continuation of earthly life.

Many scholars would date the latter part of Daniel, with its strong teaching on judgment and the contrast of eternal life and eternal shame, during the Maccabean period of the second century BC. Whether or not this is the case, it is clear that it was during this period, with its persecutions and wars, that ideas of resurrection, and in particular of the vindication of the just, came to take on a high importance in Israel's faith. An expectation grew that the coming of Messiah would be the occasion of the general resurrection.[8]

The NT gives much more prominence to resurrection and eternal life than does the OT. Here the paradigm of resurrection is, of course, that of Jesus. It is worth remarking that it is as human, not as God, that Jesus is raised. In his most extended teaching on the subject, (1 Cor 15) Paul wrote to Christians who were concerned for those who had died before the return of Christ. Here Paul refers to Jesus as 'the first fruits of those who have died.' (15.20) His resurrection presages and makes possible the general resurrection yet to come, but it is not different from that resurrection in kind. Paul chooses not to attempt to explain the mystery of resurrection in detailed terms, but in vv 35–44 piles image upon image to call his readers' confidence back to their under-

---

8 See 2 Maccabees 12.39–45 for a worked-out consequence of this expectation, as Judas Maccabeus prays for the forgiveness of fallen Jewish soldiers in the light of the coming resurrection.

standing of the resurrection of Christ for which he has established evidence and significance in vv 3–8. If we are to understand the resurrection which we look forward to, then we should look back to the resurrection of Jesus.

What, then, are the significant characteristics of this resurrection which distinguish it from the 'survival' view criticized above?

1. It recognizes the reality of death prior to resurrection. There is no suggestion in the NT that Jesus' death on the cross was anything other than a real extinction of life, leaving his friends bereft and confused.
2. It acknowledges a definite act of God. A concordance search of the NT in NRSV produces 12 verses which refer to Jesus *rising* from the dead in contrast with 41 which speak of Jesus *being raised* by God. The same balance is true in reference to believers—we read more of being raised than of rising.
3. It speaks of a transforming but physical resurrection. Jesus' body after Easter remains physical, but within a new definition of what being physical means. The evidence of continuity is there in that Jesus is recognizable (sometimes!) and that the marks of the crucifixion remain. Yet his transformation is seen in that he now seems able to be mistaken for another. The evidence of his physicality is made plain in the repeated motif of his sharing meals with the disciples, and in his offer (not taken up) to Thomas to feel his wounds. Yet at the same time his physicality has been redefined. He is able to appear and disappear in locked rooms as he chooses, and it is this physical body which ascends into the clouds, not some spiritual image.[9] Paul seems to be attempting to address the mystery of this in that chapter, 1 Cor 15, with his image of the seed falling into the ground to fulfil its potential by being changed; the identity of seed and plant is assured, but the nature of one is clearly distinct from that of the other.

This means that our preaching (not only at funerals, but especially there!) must acknowledge the reality and gravity of death before we can speak of its conquest. We must avoid any reference to eternal life which encourages hearers to see it as anything other than an active gift of God. The hope we have warrant to proclaim is that of resurrection to a life continuous with this earthly life, yet transformed by grace.[10] The reliable model for our own hope of resur-

---

9   Note that the raising of Lazarus is not of the same kind as the resurrection of Jesus. Jesus was raised to a new, eternal life. Lazarus was restored to his former life. In a sense, the raising of Lazarus was the undoing of death, and changed Lazarus. The resurrection of Jesus was the conquest of death, and changed the world.

10   There is the question of the 'intermediate state' of the dead between the moment of death and the Resurrection. On this, the biblical witness seems unclear. Jesus' promise to the thief on the cross of 'today in paradise' (Lk 23.43) seems to conflict with the picture we derive from Revelation of the saints awaiting the *parousia* with barely-restrained impatience (Rev 6.9ff)! What we can be clear about is that the final picture of heaven is one of a 'new heaven and a new earth' (Rev 21.1). All that is in between is complicated by the tension between the expected Resurrection of all and the actual Resurrection of one man on the first Easter Day. The period in which we live and die is one of eschatological tension, where all is not clear!

rection is that of Jesus, and it is to him that we must point mourners both as the means to resurrection and as the key to understanding what it may mean.

The Communion of Saints

There is a second aspect to the Christian hope, which at times runs counter to the strong eschatological emphasis above. Under the principal biblical theme of a resurrection at the end of time is the concept that there is an ongoing fellowship of the faithful departed. Heb 11 is often said to reflect this, though the writer's meaning is clearly that the witnesses are those whose life and faith testify to us of the faithfulness of God.[11]

What we need to guard against in drawing upon this side of Christian hope is, again, a popular half-understanding. To speak too easily of a shared fellowship in heaven with those who have gone before us can lead to a feeling that eternity will be more or less a continuation of what has begun here, with relationships taken up where we left off at death. Counter to this, we need to bear in mind Jesus' words in response to the Sadducees' question about the resurrection (Luke 20.27–40). On the one hand, this passage deals specifically with the resurrection, but we may legitimately presume that the 'interim' state of life beyond death has features in common. There is surely no negation of human love in the resurrection, but there is clearly a transformation of the expression of that love, such that relationships will not simply 'carry over.'

The communion of saints is a profound expression of the Christian belief that our worship and discipleship take place in the context of a worshipping community. That community stretches not only spatially across the world but temporally and metaphysically with those who are our brothers and sisters but who have lived and died before us. It is a development of the belief that our worship on earth reflects and participates in the continuing and perfect worship of the angels about God's throne. As such, it is a truth expressed above all when *we* pray and worship, and is dependent upon the drawing together of individual human lives within the life of God. It may be encouraging, but it is not necessarily comfortable!

We have, then, a dual-focussed hope. The emphasis is upon a future, transformative resurrection, but there is an undercurrent of affirming our current fellowship with the 'faithful departed' in the communion of saints. How, then, can we begin to proclaim this hope in a manner which is both authentic and appropriate? There are distinct aspects of the service which we have at our disposal, and they should be used carefully together. We turn to them now.

---

11   It is 'what we see in them, not what they see in us, that is the writer's main point' (J Moffatt, *A Critical and Exegetical Commentary on the Epistle to the Hebrews* [Clark, 1924] p 193) It may be worthy of note that most of the New Testament's tendencies to hold a metaphysical dualism alongside an eschatological arise in the letter to the Hebrews. This may relate to the way in which the author writes here.

5

The Tribute—Making it Personal

The CW funeral provides for the practice, increasingly popular in some areas and communities, of a friend or relative 'saying a few words' about the deceased. This is almost universally done in funerals covered by television or film, be they real or (more often) fictional. As many people are exposed to the pastoral offices of the church primarily through TV, there can be a pressure of expectation on mourners that someone will speak in this vein. In my experience it is worth reassuring people early in the planning of the funeral that, while a personal tribute may add much to the funeral service, it is not required.

The structure of the service deliberately provides for this tribute to take place early on, distinguishing it clearly from the sermon in its place and purpose. The tribute is by its nature backward-looking, and so belongs in the former part of the funeral's progression.

> Remembering and honouring the life of the person who has died, and the evidence of God's grace and work in them, should be done in the earlier part of the service, after the opening prayer, though if occasion demands it may be woven into the sermon or come immediately before the Commendation. It may be done in conjunction with the placing of symbols, and may be spoken by a family member or friend or by the minister using information provided by the family. It is preferable not to interrupt the flow of the reading(s) and sermon with a tribute of this kind.[12]

If a tribute is to be made, advice is necessary. Firstly, it is important that the tribute is offered by the right person. Clearly it should ideally be someone who knew the deceased well, but a member of the immediate family may not be ideal. He or she may well find the whole experience too emotional, either breaking down at the lectern or finding that they are unable properly to grieve at the funeral because of the pressure not to let the family down by failing to speak their words.

If the church has a well-established team of bereavement visitors, it may be that some would be willing to spend the time with the family to build up a rounded picture of the deceased, and then to speak as a 'church friend' on behalf of the mourners. This would bring a considerable burden of preparation and expectation, but where it is possible it might be a valuable aspect to that pastoral relationship, and have long-term benefits.

Once the speaker has been chosen, I have found in my own ministry that the following points help.

12 *Pastoral Services,* p 291, Note 4.

1. Ask to meet with the speaker, or at least discuss the tribute by telephone.
2. Be clear in your own mind how long can be allowed for the tribute. In a service in church followed by burial in the churchyard, time may not be of the essence. At a full service in the crematorium, any more than two or three minutes is likely to cause timing problems later in the service. Most people unaccustomed to public speaking find it hard to gauge the time taken to read a text, so I have found it better to suggest a limit to the number of words (normally at about 100 per minute) which allows some leeway for overrun.
3. Ask for a full-text copy of the tribute in advance. One reason is to be able to suggest any necessary amendments—while this is a personal reflection, it is in the context of a solemn public service, and some recollections may be best left for the gathering afterward! Another is in order that content may be checked against anything which you plan to say yourself during the course of the service.
4. Ensure that the speaker is clear about the practical details—when the tribute comes in the service, how it may be signalled by the minister, where to speak, whether to use a microphone, whether it will be switched on…
5. With a full-text copy of the tribute in hand, it is possible to offer the reassurance that, if the speaker should be unable to complete what he/she has planned to say due to emotional strain, you will continue where he/she has left off. I have found that this assurance generally reduces the level of tension to a point at which the speaker is more likely to be able to cope.
6. If possible, meet the speaker just before the service begins, even at the church gate, for reassurance.

More often, I have found that mourners will prefer to ask the minister to 'say a few words for us.' Sometimes, at the funeral of a well-known member of the congregation, this will feel natural and appropriate. More often, the words can feel forced and superficial, to the speaker if (hopefully) not to the hearers. Where one's first contact with the family is on the notification of death, then one is aware of receiving a very partial view of the deceased. I use 'partial' here both in its sense of being incomplete and in that of being biased, usually in a more favourable direction than may have been the case during life!

In preparing for any funeral, I have found it helpful to gather as much information as possible about the deceased without turning a pastoral visit into an interrogation with a clipboard. I find that asking to see a photograph helps me to imagine the deceased in life. It also tends to open up avenues of conversation which lead into details of a shared life and relationship. I try to be clear with the mourners that I am asking about the deceased mainly for my own understanding, so that they know not to expect from me a chronicle of a life. If it emerges that the mourners know a member of the church congregation, that person may well be able to add some recollections and impressions which will enrich your picture of the deceased.

One thing which it is vital to find out and use is the name by which the deceased was generally known. Funeral directors will generally provide the 'official' name, but in some cases this name was last used at a baptism or a marriage. There are many possible abbreviations of formal names ('Margaret' could easily have been known as Maggie, Peggy or Madge depending on the area). There are also those cases where a completely different name has been used throughout life ('Albert' may have been known to everyone at work as Bob). Most people will regard the inappropriate use of a formal name as excusable (unlike using the wrong name altogether!) but it will jar and increase the impression that the minister has been brought in to do a job, rather than caring about the deceased and the mourners.

In other aspects, where I have been asked to do all of the speaking, I have tried to be specific so far as my own experience (if any) of the deceased goes, but general beyond that. This does not provide a safeguard against gaffes— the mourners may have omitted to mention whole areas of the deceased's life, even down to honours, convictions or prior families. It does, though, avoid the sense of falseness which most of us project when describing someone we never met as if we had known them well. An invitation to the congregation to consider their own memories can help the sense of honesty, that the minister is there to help those who mourn to grieve in their own way, not to lead them into a particular way of doing so. An example might be 'I've been told of Don's infectious laugh. Perhaps many of you might remember times when it carried you along.' Or 'I've seen some of the results of Jane's love for her garden, still flowering now. Maybe you know from your own memories how much it meant to her.'

Sometimes it can be appropriate for the minister to say a few words about the deceased at the beginning of the service, settling people in with the reassurance that we know for whom we are here. Sometimes it will be more suitable for some personal notes to be woven into the sermon. In this case, it is more important than ever that the biblical reading is chosen with the specific person in mind. An appropriate reading gives opportunity to the preacher to express the gospel in a way that feels personal to the deceased without having to be contrived or forced.

6

The Sermon—Proclaiming the Gospel

The purpose of the sermon is clearly distinguished from that of any tribute.

> The purpose of the sermon is to proclaim the gospel in the context of the death of this particular person.[13]

Provided that we see the nature of preaching as relating both to text and to situation, then one vital step in preparing to preach is the choice of the text.

Choosing Readings

The rubrics of the service require at least one NT reading, and provide as an option for another from either Testament. A selection of 'recommended' readings is given,[14] on which there are some comments below. It is, of course, possible to choose any other biblical texts. The questions we must ask are, though, the same whether we choose from the recommended list or from elsewhere. They relate to the two aspects of the stated purpose of the sermon.

1. Does this passage provide opportunity to proclaim the gospel in an authentic interpretation?
2. Does this passage relate in some way to the life of the deceased?

On the first question, it may be important sometimes to go one step further. If there is a particular issue in the mourners' understanding of the gospel, it may at times be appropriate to choose a text which gently challenges their understanding. On the other hand, it may be pastorally appropriate to choose one which supports them in those aspects of their understanding which are correct, and to look for other opportunities to point them in a new and better direction.

On this second point, an example might help. I have found 1 Cor 15 to fit naturally into the funeral of anyone who had a particular interest in agriculture or gardening, with its imagery of the seed falling into the ground to grow into a plant of appropriate kind. This was a part of that person's experience which we can now use to help us to understand what we are about at a funeral. This is perhaps the clearest case of such a link, and we need to guard against becoming contrived or indulgent. A link between an aspect of the character of God and that of the deceased, for example, should probably not be pressed too far! What we are looking for is for hearers to recognize something

13 *Pastoral Services*, p 291, Note 5.
14 *Pastoral Services*, pp 383–391.

familiar in the passage which feels appropriate for the one they have come to mourn. The possibilities, though, are many.

A necessary caution is that this approach risks laziness, so that the same funeral sermon 'will do' for any keen gardener. Bear in mind that many people will attend a number of successive funerals at which you preach, and the impression of a personal and appropriate sermon will quickly be dispelled if all that changes each time is the name. With this proviso in mind, I offer a few comments on those readings which are printed in full. *Pastoral Services*, pp 390–391, provide a much longer list of recommended readings and psalms which may well be of use in finding the text appropriate to the situation.

John 6.35–40

This passage looks strongly to the general resurrection 'on the last day,' by the will of the Father through Jesus. Combined with the reference to the Bread of Life, this passage would work well for a funeral within a Communion service, celebrating the life of a committed and communicant Christian. On the other hand, it is a passage which stresses the openness of the invitation to salvation—'anyone who comes to me I will never drive away.' This may be a comfort to those whose loved ones died in a less than perfect state, but there is some risk that the language will become confused in hearers' minds with the popular concept that death is in itself a 'going to God.' Thus care should be taken to avoid an easy universalism.

Looking for personal links, it might be appropriate to use this of anyone the positive aspects of whose life centred around providing for others.

John 11.17–27

The raising of Lazarus is a particularly vivid story for use at a funeral, but one which has its own risks.

This passage points us again towards 'the resurrection on the last day' and includes the words which traditionally herald the beginning of the funeral service, 'I am the resurrection and the life…' So there are powerful promises here. The risk, though, is twofold. On one level, and particularly for an 'untimely' death, there may well be a sense of resentment. 'After all, if Jesus could raise Lazarus from death, why did not he do anything for my wife?' It would seem incautious to use this story without ensuring that this issue is addressed. A second level of risk is that of confusing the resurrection for which we hope with the raising of Lazarus. As commented above (footnote 9) this raising is of a kind entirely different from the resurrection. It may be grasped by grieving relatives as an example of the restoration of a family relationship, which is not the substance of our hope.

So far as personal appropriateness goes, then perhaps this might be useful where the focus could be on relatives in their grief, but the caution above must be noted.

John 14.1–6

This passage combines the reassurance of Jesus' promise with the challenge that it is only through him that this promise can be realized. The promise and the challenge can be balanced according to the needs of the congregation. The emphasis of this text on Christ's very personal guidance through death to a place prepared for us can come across very powerfully. This is so especially when at the funeral of a committed Christian it is possible to make a link between a life walking with Jesus and passing through death with Jesus' guidance. Thomas' question 'How can we know the way?' opens any number of possibilities for pointing the congregation towards God.

The 'journeying' sense of this passage and the uncertainty of Thomas' question speak well to those whose faith has been genuine but unclear. They can also be appropriate for those whose lives have been characterized by some confusion and upheaval, or constant movement and travel. From a very different angle, I have found that the idea of 'many dwelling places' in the Father's house seems appropriate for those whose lives have been particularly individual. We can emphasize that God has a distinct place prepared for each distinct individual in his house, and easily ask a congregation to imagine what the deceased would have needed to furnish such a room, prepared for eternity. This does need an element of caution, though, as it tends to lead to the assumption that the deceased is definitely ensconced in such a dwelling.

Romans 8.31–end

This text focuses not so much on the resurrection as on the confidence we may have in the surrounding and sustaining love of God through Jesus, from which nothing can separate us. In preaching, it may help to draw attention to v 32, that this love is mediated through God's gift of his Son. Without the substance of this reminder, such an assurance of divine love in the face of death and loss may seem hollow. The long list of things which cannot come between us and God is eloquent in itself, and may warrant rereading and applying as much as preaching.

The reference to God as Father giving up his child may, in the right circumstances, help those who have lost children themselves, but only if very sensitively handled. The emphasis could, perhaps, be upon the truth that God, therefore, knows what it is to lose a son. The powerful emphasis through the passage on the unstoppable nature of God's love may touch those who have seen the deceased struggle, against illness or force of circumstance. On the other hand, it may be a beginning of comfort to those who feel that they have lost their main source and object of human love, a husband or wife perhaps. The assurance that there is a God who continues to love them is good news.

1 Corinthians (a) 15.1–26, 35–38, 42–44a, 53–end; (b) 15.20–end

(b) was the one reading provided for the BCP burial service, and was provided in shorter form in ASB by the selection of verses in (a), but beginning from v 20. Both selections root the Christian hope firmly in the resurrection of Jesus. (a) does more to establish the reality and importance of this event, (b) places more emphasis on the implications of the resurrection for living out Christian faith in this life. Both rebuke those who would ask too many questions about the nature of the resurrection body, and provide a wealth of images which could be used to point hearers towards elements of our hope.

The greatest weakness of both texts is their length, at 784 and 868 words respectively. A reading of 7–9 minutes would challenge the attention-span of most regular church congregations, and seems unlikely to be appropriate even in a church funeral where enough time has been allowed. There is simply no way that these readings could be used in their entirety in a crematorium chapel with a 30-minute turnaround. That said, the note on readings does say that one of the recommended texts should *normally* be used, so perhaps circumstances might allow a careful editing of these texts to retain the elements which would be most useful in any given funeral situation.

I have mentioned earlier that this text can be appropriate to anyone used to the life of plants. It has, though, a much wider relevance and importance in that it uses a concrete image—that of the seed and the plant—to address what can be an abstract idea of the resurrection. The image of the sprouting seed is one which many may remember after the funeral, and the link to the natural cycle of the year provides for a recurring positive reminder of resurrection each spring.

1 Thessalonians 4.13–end

Paul is clear here about the nature of resurrection as hope for the living, rooted in Jesus' death and rising. The stress, as with much of this letter, is on the anticipation of the general resurrection and the reuniting of saints living and dead in Christ.

A strength of this passage is for those who long to be reunited with the deceased. The new meeting is placed clearly in the act of God, but is anticipated with joy. The main weakness I have found with this text is that the image of being 'caught up in the clouds...to meet the Lord in the air' is not one which people seem to find easy to appreciate. For some reason there is a bit more of a credibility gap to bridge here than with some other images of resurrection.

Revelation 21.1-7

The focus here is entirely away from the resurrection of the individual to the consummation of resurrection with the establishment of a new heaven and new earth. The proclamation of this new world is in powerful tone, and comes with the announcement that suffering is no more. There may be a need in preaching from this passage to avoid an easy 'so everything's going to be all right' message, but the majesty of the passage deserves to be heard, and to bring hope and comfort to those who mourn.

Above all, this passage seems appropriate to those whose journey to death has been a difficult one, where the promise of an end to pain and crying is an integral part of hope for the life to come. It seems appropriate for those whose separation from the deceased is most painful. The tender promise of the wiping away of tears balances the force of the promise that death will, at last, be defeated.

Text to Sermon

Once the text is chosen, the usual questions of sermon planning arise, complicated by the special demands of the funeral context. One question is the amount of time available and appropriate for a sermon. Where the entire funeral is in a crematorium chapel, the key question is likely to be how much time is possible. Each successive revision of the funeral liturgy seems to lengthen it, and even omitting all optional material, the CW order is likely to fill the time available in many crematoria with 30-minute bookings. Depending upon the choice of hymn(s) etc, and any personal elements which mourners wish to include in the service, the time available for the sermon could easily be squeezed to 3 minutes. This will probably allow only one point to be made properly, with an element of personal reference built in.

Where the funeral takes place in church, more flexibility is possible. If the committal is at the crematorium or a cemetery, then it will be necessary to ensure that the funeral director has allowed enough time for the service planned. If the burial is in the churchyard, then more flexibility and spontaneity may be possible. Then the issue becomes that of how long is appropriate for this congregation. Bear in mind that the sermon will normally be a time of passivity in the middle of a service where mourners want to *do* something. Unless the sermon relates to their need and to the life of the deceased, the time available before frustration sets in is likely to be short.

Compounding this limit on the content we can include is the recognition that some of the mourners will have little or no concept of Christian belief. Others will have their ability to take in the message impaired by their emotions. This means that the sermon must be in simple, preferably concrete terms, with as little as possible assumed.

It is important, also, to remember on whom we are concentrating the message of the sermon—usually this will be on the needs of the immediate family, but sometimes it may be a wider group. An example might be when a member of the congregation dies, his or her family not being Christians. It is important then to recognize the needs of more than one group. In that situation, Christian friends need a celebration of victory in Christ, while family and other friends may not recognize the person spoken of by a minister who has known the deceased well, but only in the particular context of church life. In another case, the deceased's family may be divided, and have very different feelings and needs. The right balance must be struck in each case.

It is surely a counsel of perfection to ask that ministers produce sermons,

21

perhaps several times each week, which in 3-6 minutes manage to explain the gospel hope in a way that is personal, pastoral and challenging. In practice, the gospel hope which we proclaim on the basis of a given text will not vary much from one funeral to another. Perhaps many ministers will develop a 'modular' style of funeral preaching, choosing text and so message as appropriate to individual funerals from a number of 'core' messages and tailoring these to the unique situation. Whether we are working with five funerals a week or one a month, if we are clear about the nature of the hope we are attempting to communicate, and clear about how we can relate that hope to the bereaved people before us, we will have much more chance of using well those few minutes available to us.

7

Sermon and Service

The message we preach is not expressed only by the words on the page. Those words are reinforced or contradicted by the rest of our service in both senses of the term—our loving service of pastoral care and the liturgical service of the funeral, of which the sermon is but one part.

Clearly the message received by a grieving family will depend upon the care they have received from the church's representatives, as well as upon the words spoken by one of those representatives at the funeral. Good and creative use of the structured progression of services supplied by CW and other sources will help here, as will the sense of the church's support through the time of the funeral. In the final analysis, though, it is the degree of care which mourners feel they have received which will have the greatest influence upon the hearing that is given to the message which is preached.

The liturgical setting of the sermon will also have a great effect. Possibilities will depend upon the location of the funeral and the nature of the building in use, but aspects to consider may include the following.

1. Where will the coffin be placed? In a crematorium chapel there is unlikely to be an option, but it is still important to be aware of the arrangement of minister, catafalque (coffin stand) and congregation.
2. Where will the minister sit or stand for different elements of the service? Think through the different effects of speaking to the family over the coffin, standing by it or standing on the opposite side of the church. There is no 'right' approach, but different funerals may require different arrangements. My own strong conviction is, though, that staying tied to a lectern

throughout does not enhance the congregation's understanding of what is going on. Movement is important, especially in a service which has its own sense of movement from death to life.

3. What, if any, visual and personal symbols will be used? There is provision in the service for the placing of personal symbols, and this will need careful planning and, perhaps, restriction. There is also opportunity for the placing of cross and Bible on the coffin. I have found that many mourners value being able to come forward and place a flower on the coffin just before the committal, and other possibilities will occur to other ministers.

4. What, if any, sacramental aspect should there be? Where we commend a faithful Christian to God, the CW funeral fits well into the Eucharist, and a full order for such a service is provided. Where someone has been a regular communicant, and where the mourners are themselves Christians, such a service is entirely appropriate, and a proper and powerful expression of our belief in the communion of saints worshipping in heaven as on earth. At a less structural and committed level, there is provision for the sprinkling of the coffin with water, speaking symbolically of the individual's baptism into the people of God and the body of Christ. Where these sacramental signs can be used honestly, they can have considerable power.

5. What do hymns contribute to the service? Some are perennials at a funeral, often for good reason (*Crimond* and *Abide with me* spring to mind) but it may be useful to have one's own list of possible hymns to discuss with mourners. Unless you are a confident singer to introduce the first few lines, it may even help to have the choir or music group produce a tape of first verses, so that people recognize the hymns being discussed. It is, of course, vital that hymns sung at a funeral are well-known. As with the sermon, it is also worth looking at hymns for the nature of the hope that they proclaim and for any personal appropriateness. Further, it helps if hymns can be placed so that their 'mood' fits the part of the service in which they are sung. So a hymn of assurance in time of trial may appropriately be placed early on, one of the hope of resurrection later. To insert hymns at points where they do not 'fit' can disrupt the whole sense of progression of the service.

6. Are any non-biblical (Christian or secular) readings to be used? If so, do they fit with the sermon or (particularly if chosen by the mourners) go directly against its tenor? When should they be used, and by whom should they be read? Again, the flow of the service may well dictate the proper point for the use of a particular reading.

There will often be something of a 'balancing act' between the demands of available time, the preferences of relatives and the minister's sense of the progression and tone of the service. But within the constraints which apply, it is vital to keep sight of the funeral both as a whole in itself and as a part of the whole process of giving liturgical expression to grieving.

8

Conclusion

The need for funeral ministry is not about to go away. The proportion of children baptized continues to fall, and marriage (where it happens at all) may be at least as likely to take place in a hotel or stately home as in a church. Anecdotal evidence, though, suggests that the decline in 'Christian' funerals has been much slower. For as long as churches and ministers provide good pastoral care and appropriate liturgy, that situation will continue. For as long as it continues, those of us who lead funerals have an opportunity to help people in one of their darkest times with words of real hope which may last beyond the resolution of their immediate sorrow.

9

Further Reading

On the Common Worship funeral provision
Pastoral Services (Church House, 2000)
New Handbook of Pastoral Liturgy by Michael Perham (SPCK, 2000)
Using Common Worship—Funerals by R Anne Horton (Praxis/CHP, 2000)

Related Grove Booklets
P56   *The Pain of Parting* by David Howell
W142   *Prayer and the Departed* by Christopher Cocksworth
W160   *Dying and Death: the New Services* by Trevor Lloyd
B11   *New Heavens, New Earth* by Tom Wright

On funeral ministry and pastoral care generally
Funerals and How to Improve Them by Tony Walter (Hodders, 1990)